Killer Snakes

Diamondback Rattlesnake

By Autumn Leigh

Gareth Stevens
Publishing

Please visit our Web site, www.garethstevens.com. For a free color catalog of all our high-quality books, call toll free 1-800-542-2595 or fax 1-877-542-2596.

Library of Congress Cataloging-in-Publication Data

Leigh, Autumn.
Diamondback rattlesnake / Autumn Leigh.
     p. cm. — (Killer snakes)
Includes index.
ISBN 978-1-4339-4548-9 (pbk.)
ISBN 978-1-4339-4549-6 (6-pack)
ISBN 978-1-4339-4547-2 (library binding)
1. Eastern diamondback rattlesnake—Juvenile literature. 2. Western diamondback rattlesnake—Juvenile literature. I. Title.
QL666.O69L45 2011
597.96'38—dc22

                              2010030697

First Edition

Published in 2011 by
Gareth Stevens Publishing
111 East 14th Street, Suite 349
New York, NY 10003

Copyright © 2011 Gareth Stevens Publishing

Designer: Michael J. Flynn
Editor: Greg Roza

Photo credits: Cover, pp. 1, (2–4, 6, 8, 10, 12, 14, 16, 18, 20–24 snake skin texture), 5, 7, 9, 11, 13, 15, 17, 19, 21 Shutterstock.com.

Printed in the United States of America

CPSIA compliance information: Batch #CW11GS: For further information contact Gareth Stevens, New York, New York at 1-800-542-2595.

Contents

Boldface words appear in the glossary.

Deadly Diamondbacks

Diamondback rattlesnakes are often called diamondbacks. They are excellent hunters. They use **venom** to kill. Diamondbacks are pit **vipers**. Pit vipers have small openings called "pits" below their eyes. These openings sense heat, which helps pit vipers find food.

5

East and West

In the United States, there are two types of diamondbacks. Eastern diamondbacks live in the Southeast. Western diamondbacks live in the Southwest. Both kinds have sharp **fangs** and rattles on their tails.

western diamondback

eastern diamondback

7

The eastern diamondback is the largest venomous snake in the United States. Most adults are about 5 feet (1.5 m) long and weigh about 5 pounds (2.3 kg). However, they can be up to 8 feet (2.4 m) long and weigh up to 10 pounds (4.5 kg). The western diamondback is smaller and less venomous.

eastern diamondback

9

Shades and Shapes

Most diamondbacks are black, gray, and brown. They can also be red, yellow, and green. Diamondbacks have diamond shapes on their backs, which is how they got their name. Western diamondbacks have black-and-white stripes on their tails.

11

Baby Diamondbacks

Female diamondbacks commonly have babies every other summer. They can have between 5 and 20 babies at one time. Baby diamondbacks are born with fangs that can shoot venom. This helps them against enemies. Their mother leaves as soon as they are born.

13

A Snake That Rattles

Snakes **shed** their skin as they grow larger. However, every time a rattlesnake sheds its skin, a tiny piece remains on the tip of its tail. When these pieces build up, a rattle grows. A diamondback shakes its rattle to warn enemies to stay away.

rattle

Diamondback Attack!

Diamondbacks eat rats, mice, rabbits, birds, and other small animals. A diamondback's colors and markings help it hide. It uses its pits to sense the heat of a passing animal. When an animal is close by, the diamondback **attacks**!

17

When a diamondback attacks, it raises the front of its body off the ground. It bites and uses its fangs to shoot venom into the animal's body. The venom puts the animal to sleep or kills it. Once the animal stops moving, the rattlesnake swallows it whole!

19

Diamondbacks and People

Diamondbacks stay away from people. However, they sometimes attack when they are surprised. Diamondback venom hurts the blood system and kills body **tissues**. The venom is very painful and can result in death. If you ever hear a diamondback's rattle, stay away!

Snake Facts
Eastern Diamondback Rattlesnake

Length	5 feet (1.5 m) some grow to 8 feet (2.4 m)
Weight	5 pounds (2.3 kg) larger snakes can weigh 10 pounds (4.5 kg)
Where It Lives	southeastern United States
Life Span	10 to 20 years
Killer Fact	Adult diamondbacks can control how much venom they shoot into an animal. They may warn a larger animal to stay away by giving it a "dry" bite with no venom at all.

Glossary

attack: to try to harm someone or something

fang: a sharp tooth

shed: to get rid of something

tissue: matter that forms the parts of living things

venom: something a snake makes in its body that can harm other animals

viper: a venomous snake

For More Information

Books

Gunderson, Megan M. *Diamondback Rattlesnakes.* Edina, MN: ABDO Publishing, 2011.

White, Nancy. *Diamondback Rattlers: America's Most Venomous Snakes!* New York, NY: Bearpoint Publishing, 2009.

Web Sites

Animal Fact Sheet: Western Diamondback Rattlesnake
www.desertmuseum.org/kids/oz/long-fact-sheets/ Diamondback%20Rattlesnake.php
Read more about the western diamondback rattlesnake.

Eastern Diamondback Rattlesnake
animals.nationalgeographic.com/animals/reptiles/ eastern-diamondback-rattlesnake/
Read more about the eastern diamondback rattlesnake.

Index